CORNERSTO
OF FREEDC

THE BRANCHES OF U.S. GOVERNMENT

BY MICHAEL BURGAN

CHILDREN'S PRESS®
An Imprint of Scholastic Inc.
New York   Toronto   London   Auckland   Sydney
Mexico City   New Delhi   Hong Kong
Danbury, Connecticut

BRINGING HISTORY to LIFE

Library of Congress Cataloging-in-Publication Data
Burgan, Michael.
  The Branches of U.S. Government/by Michael Burgan.
     p. cm.—(Cornerstones of freedom)
  Includes bibliographical references and index.
  ISBN-13: 978-0-531-25028-0 (lib. bdg.)   ISBN-10: 0-531-25028-8 (lib. bdg.)
  ISBN-10: 978-0-531-26553-6 (pbk.)   ISBN-13: 0-531-26553-6 (pbk.)
  1. United States—Politics and government—Juvenile literature.
  2. Separation of powers—United States—Juvenile literature. I. Title.
  II. Series.
  JK40.B87 2011
  320.473—dc22   2011011287

Photographs © 2012: Alamy Images: 16 (Rob Crandall/SCPhotos), 41 (rudy
k); AP Images: 47 (Asharq-al Awsat), 55 (Pablo Martinez Monsivais),
6 (North Wind Picture Archives), 42 (Evan Vucci), 4 top, 40, 50; Corbis
Images: back cover (Patsy Lynch/Retna Ltd.), cover (Rudy Sulgan); Everett
Collection, Inc./Kristin Callahan: 28; Getty Images: 26 (Andrew Harrer/
Bloomberg), 48 (Jay Mallin/Bloomberg), 22 (Ethan Miller), 34 (Tim Sloan/
AFP), 45 (USAF), 54 (Jim Watson/AFP); iStockphoto: 49 (Dave Newman),
19 (Alice Scully); Library of Congress: 20 (Thomas Hamilton Crawford),
12, 56 bottom (Peter S. Duval/C.S. Williams), 21 (Harris & Ewing), 33, 58
...ational Photo Co./Underwood & Underwood), 37 (Robert Matthew
.../Corcoran Gallery of Art, Washington, D.C.), 2, 3, 38 (United Press
...tional); Michael Burgan: 64; North Wind Picture Archives: 14,
...top; ShutterStock, Inc./iofoto: 4 bottom, 25; Superstock, Inc./
...rnet: 46, 57; The Granger Collection, New York: 5 bottom, 8,
...Image Works: 39 (akg-images), 5 top, 29 (Rob Crandall), 51
...0 (Robert Edge Pine/H. Armstrong Roberts/ClassicStock),
...), 13 (John Trumbull/Iberfoto), 23 (Jim West).

Did you know that studying history can be fun?

BRING HISTORY TO LIFE by becoming a history investigator. Examine the evidence (primary and secondary source materials); cross-examine the people and witnesses. Take a look at what was happening at the time—but be careful! What happened years ago might suddenly become incredibly interesting and change the way you think!

Contents

Meeting in Philadelphia

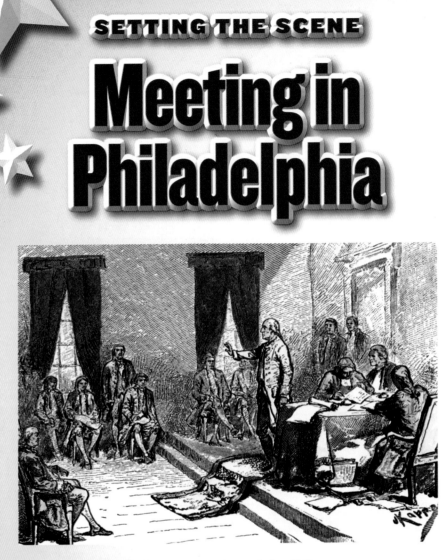

The Constitutional Convention shaped the U.S. government as we know it today.

Some of America's greatest men met in Philadelphia's State House during the summer of 1787. Their states had sent them there as **delegates** to a special convention. The 55 delegates were all white male property owners. They debated what kind of government the United States should have.

Some of the men believed sovereignty should rest with the states. Sovereignty, or supreme power to rule, would make the states independent. They could join together to pursue common goals. But no other government or power would be above them.

Others thought sovereignty rested with the American people as citizens of the United States. These delegates were led by James Madison of Virginia. They wanted to create a strong national government. It would share power with the states. But the states would not be totally independent.

Madison and his supporters were called nationalists, or Federalists. Their arguments mostly won out. The delegates created a strong U.S. government with the U.S. Constitution. This **federal** government received its sovereignty from the people. Madison argued for spreading it among three distinct branches. He called this concept separation of powers. The branches would be the **legislative**, the **executive**, and the **judicial**. Each branch would have specific rights and duties. Each branch would also limit or approve what another branch did. This was known as checks and balances. One branch of government checked, or limited, the power of another. Each tried to balance out the power of the others.

CHAPTER 1

CREATING A NEW GOVERNMENT

The American colonies gained independence from Great Britain in the American Revolution.

ON APRIL 19, 1775, IN Lexington, Massachusetts, the American Revolution began. For a decade, Americans had increasingly resisted efforts by Great Britain to tax them and limit their settlement in the West. The British claimed the right to rule over their American colonies as they wanted. Those opposing views led to the revolution. They also led to the Americans announcing their independence in the Declaration of Independence in 1776.

The Continental Congress was an early version of what would become the U.S. government.

The 13 American colonies had become independent states. They were united in the effort to win their freedom from Great Britain. Delegates from the states met in Philadelphia, Pennsylvania, in 1775 to form the Second Continental Congress. This Congress knew the states needed a national government to carry out the war against Great Britain. But many members feared the power of a strong central government. Congress finally wrote the Articles of Confederation between 1776 and 1777. They made Congress itself the government for the United States. The states approved the document in 1781.

The Articles of Confederation said that the states would "enter into a firm league of friendship with each other." Each state kept its independence and had one vote in Congress. Each state had to approve **amendments** for them to pass.

The Three Functions of Government

Most of the leaders who would create the U.S. government agreed by 1776 that any government had three basic functions. One was to make laws. One was to execute, or carry out, the laws. The last was to make sure the laws were carried out fairly. These have been called the legislative, executive, and judicial functions of government.

A Boston lawyer named John Adams wrote a letter to a friend in 1776. The letter explained what he believed was the ideal form of government. Adams's government would have independent legislative, executive, and judicial branches. That separation would guarantee "a government of laws, and not of men." This meant that

John Adams

In 1770, a Boston mob protesting British taxes attacked British soldiers based in that city. The soldiers opened fire and killed five protesters. John Adams knew the citizens were angry with the British. But he also knew that the soldiers deserved a fair trial. He agreed to defend them in court. This put the idea of a government of laws, not men, into practice. Adams was one of the first Americans to call for independence from Great Britain. He was the first vice president. He was elected president in 1796.

leaders could not do whatever they chose.

The legislative branch that wrote the laws would have two houses. One would be directly elected by the people. The other would be chosen by the members of that house. The executive branch would have the power to call out the militia. The militia was the military force used by the colonies during times of emergency. The judicial branch would run the court system. They would interpret and apply the laws in certain situations, such as crimes or business disputes.

From the Articles to the Constitution

The American states won their independence from Great Britain in 1783. But some people believed that the Articles of Confederation had not created the best government for the new nation. In 1787, Adams wrote,

The Founding Fathers thought carefully about how the new nation's government should be organized.

"The people's rights and liberties . . . can never be preserved without . . . separating the executive power from the legislative." This was because the legislature's elected members best reflected what the people from a particular state wanted.

Congress soon called for a convention to meet in Philadelphia to discuss changing the Articles of

SPOTLIGHT ON

The Constitutional Convention

The Constitutional Convention took place in Philadelphia from May 25 to September 17, 1787. Every state except Rhode Island sent delegates. George Washington was chosen to lead the convention. Fifty-five delegates attended. Not all of them were in Philadelphia the entire time. Thirty-nine delegates signed the Constitution. Some had left the city before the convention ended. Some did not sign because they did not like the new government the Constitution created. One of the most discussed issues at the convention was the inclusion of an executive branch. This branch was absent from the Articles of Confederation.

Confederation. The delegates created the Constitution instead. This new document outlined an entirely new government.

James Madison wrote a detailed plan for the Constitution. His proposed government would also have a legislature with two houses. One would be a "lower" house directly elected by the people. The other would be an "upper" house chosen by members of that lower house. It was decided that the legislature would be called Congress. The delegates also created a single executive called the president. The president would be "commander in chief," or head, of the military. The constitution also called for a federal judiciary, with one supreme court and any lower courts that Congress created.

The Constitution was sent to the states to be ratified in September 1787. In 1791, a series of amendments to the Constitution called the Bill of Rights served to further check government power. The amendments spelled out basic rights that the federal government could not take away.

The Bill of Rights consists of the first ten amendments to the U.S. Constitution.

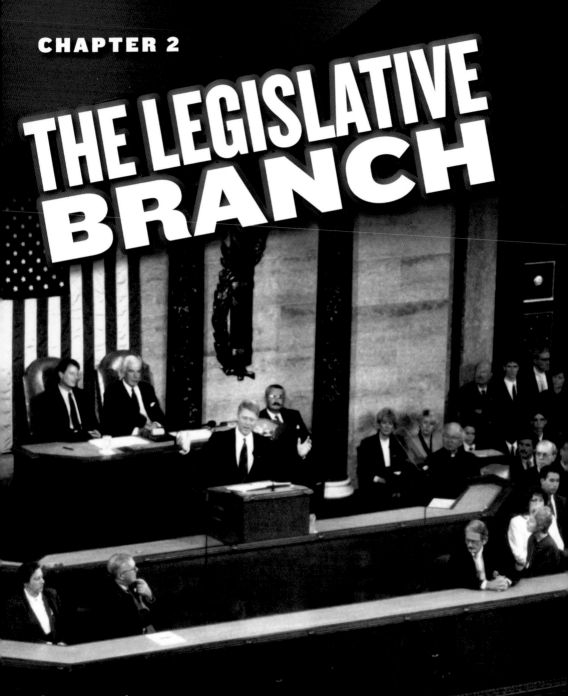

CHAPTER 2

THE LEGISLATIVE BRANCH

Congress works to create
the laws that govern the
United States.

THE DELEGATES BEGAN THE
Constitution with Article I. It describes how the
states would send members to Congress and what
each of its two houses would do. The House of
Representatives would be made up of a certain
number of representatives from each state. The
states' populations would determine how many
representatives they had. Each state would have
at least one representative. These members would
serve two-year terms and be elected by the voters.
Voting was limited at the time to free men who
owned a certain amount of property. For the Senate,
each state's lawmakers would choose two members
to represent the state. They would serve six-year
terms. Congress currently has 435 House members
and 100 senators.

Members of Congress often engage in intense debates about new laws.

What Congress Does

Each house of Congress has specific duties. **Bills** can come from either house. But only the House of Representatives can introduce bills that raise taxes. The Senate has the responsibility of approving people named by the president for certain government offices. The Senate must also approve any treaties the president makes with foreign nations. These requirements are part of the process for checking presidential power.

A bill must be approved in each house before it can be passed on to the president for review. If the House version of a bill differs from the Senate's, the two houses must make changes to one bill or the other until they are the same.

Each house also plays a role in a political process called impeachment. This process is used to remove a president or a judge who has broken the law or failed to carry out his or her duties. The House investigates to see if the accused person has actually done something wrong. The House then impeaches the person if it finds evidence. The Senate then acts like a court. It decides if the evidence is strong enough to remove the person from office.

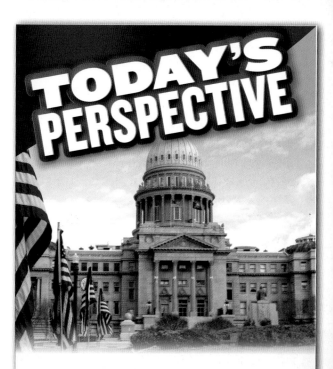

TODAY'S PERSPECTIVE

The 17th Amendment was passed in 1913. It gave voters the power to choose their senators directly. But some Americans have in recent years called for giving that power back to the state legislatures. These people say that state lawmakers will be more concerned about keeping power with the states than keeping it with federal lawmakers. The state legislatures will choose senators who reflect that view. In 2011, lawmakers in Idaho considered a proposal calling for the removal of the 17th Amendment from the Constitution, but rejected it.

The Constitution spelled out specific powers that the two houses share. Congress has the right to collect taxes and oversee business deals between the states and with foreign nations. It also has the power to declare war and to raise money for military purposes. Finally, the Constitution gives Congress the general right "to make all laws which shall be necessary and proper" for carrying out its other powers. Alexander Hamilton was one of the strongest defenders of the Constitution. He believed this general right gave Congress broad powers to address a wide range of issues. The Constitution does not have to clearly say Congress could do something, if it does not specifically deny Congress that right.

Alexander Hamilton believed in a strong federal government.

Representative Joseph G. Cannon served as Speaker of the House from 1903 to 1911.

The Constitution also defines who can be a member of Congress. A representative must be at least 25 years old and a U.S. citizen for at least seven years. Senators must be at least 30 years old and U.S. citizens for nine or more years. All members of Congress must be residents of the states they represent.

Political Parties

The House is required to have a leader called the Speaker of the House. The vice president serves as president of the Senate. But he or she only votes to break a tie.

Something the delegates did not include in the Constitution was the role of political parties. Two political parties began to form during the 1790s. One,

the Federalist Party, favored the strong federal system that Alexander Hamilton championed. It called for strengthening commerce and improving ties with Great Britain. Hamilton's Federalist Party challenged the views of the Democratic Republicans. The Democratic Republicans favored some limits on federal power. They also wanted the country to support agriculture more than commerce. James Madison and Thomas Jefferson were the leading voices of the Democratic Republicans.

The two-party system grew in importance in the following years. The party that had the most members in a house of Congress had greater control over which bills were discussed. The **majority** party also had the power to elect the Speaker of the House and the leader of the Senate. The leader of the Senate is known as the

Members of Congress, such as Carolyn Cheeks Kilpatrick from Michigan, deal with many issues affecting the people of the United States.

majority leader. Party leaders decided which of their congressional members would sit on which committees. Starting early in the 19th century, both houses set up committees to address key issues such as taxes and the military. Each committee has one person called the chairperson who directs its actions.

Congress meets at the U.S. Capitol. This building is famous for its huge dome. A model of the dome and drawings used to build it are on display at Exhibition Hall. The hall is a part of the Capitol that is open to the public. See page 60 for a link to read more information about the Capitol online.

Changes over Time

Congress maintained more power than other parts of government for many decades. But that began to change during the 20th century. A law passed in 1921 required the president to submit a **budget** for all executive departments. The lawmakers had previously worked with the separate departments to shape a budget.

Changes also took place within Congress. In 1890, Speaker of the House Thomas B. Reed pushed for rules that strengthened his power. He made it easier for votes to be called. He also gave the majority party the right to decide what bills would be discussed. Reed's Republican Party soon began using a "whip." This was a loyal party member who made sure other party members voted the way party leaders wanted. Today, both parties in both houses use whips.

Congressional leaders tried several times in the 20th century to make daily operations run more smoothly. The number of committees was reduced in 1946. During the 1970s, houses required committee chairs to be elected. The majority party member on the committee with the most years of service had previously always gotten this important job.

Another major change came toward the end of the 20th century. Party leaders, not committee chairs, often decided what bills to pursue. The Democrats and the Republicans were the two major parties. They became more **partisan**. This often makes it difficult for them to reach agreements on important issues.

Both the U.S. Senate and the U.S. House of Representatives meet in the U.S. Capitol.

CHAPTER 3

THE EXECUTIVE BRANCH

Barack Obama (right) was elected president on November 4, 2008. Joseph Biden became vice president.

THE ARTICLES OF CONFEDERATION

did not create a separate executive office. But the delegates at the Philadelphia Convention of 1787 realized that had been a mistake. They wanted to give the president enough power to carry out important duties. But they also did not want the president to have too much power to deny the sovereignty of the states and the people.

Barack Obama (left) and Joseph Biden wave to a crowd celebrating Obama's election to the presidency.

The Constitution Defines the Presidency

Article II of the Constitution outlines the executive branch. This branch includes the vice presidency and departments that help the president carry out executive duties. The president is chosen by the Electoral College. The College is made up of special electors from each state. The president must be at least 35 years old. He or she must also have been born in the United States and have been a resident of the country for at least 14 years. The president serves a four-year term. The Constitution originally did not limit the number of terms. The 22nd Amendment of 1951 set the limit at two. A president can only be removed from office by impeachment.

The first responsibility of the president listed in Article II is to serve as the commander in chief of the U.S. military. The president also commands state forces, such as the National Guard.

The president has the power to make treaties with foreign nations. Two-thirds of the Senate must approve these treaties. The Senate also has the power to reject a president's **nominees** for certain executive positions and seats on the federal courts. Some of the most important jobs go to the heads of the various executive departments that Congress created. These include the Departments of Defense, the Treasury, and Education.

SPOTLIGHT ON

The Electoral College

The Electoral College gives both voters and state legislatures a voice in presidential elections. Each state receives the same number of votes in the Electoral College as the number of members it has in Congress. Voters in each state choose their preferred presidential candidate on election day. The electors from each state then vote for the candidate who won the most votes in their state. Maine and Nebraska give voters the option to split their electoral vote if some districts prefer a different candidate. The House of Representatives then chooses the president if the electoral vote is a tie or if no candidate gets more than half of the votes. Today's candidates must receive 270 electoral votes to become president.

French academic Alexis de Tocqueville wrote a book about American society and government entitled *Democracy in America*.

The president must approve laws Congress creates. A bill goes back to Congress if the president **vetoes** it. Then the members vote on it again. The bill becomes law without the president's approval if two-thirds of the members in each house vote for it. The president generally has 10 days to act on a bill. It automatically becomes law if he or she does not accept or reject it during that time.

Political parties shape how the executive branch functions. The chance of Congress defeating a presidential veto increases when the president is from one party and Congress is controlled by the other. Party differences are another part of the system of checks and balances.

The Presidency in Action

George Washington was the first president. He had no model to follow on how to lead the executive branch. But he and Alexander Hamilton believed the executive branch should be strong and active. In 1794, some Pennsylvania farmers wanted an end to a tax on corn used to make whiskey. Their protests turned violent. Washington used the powers of militia organization granted to the president in 1792 to quickly organize troops and end the Whiskey Rebellion. Washington then used another of his executive powers to pardon the farmers who had been arrested. The president can pardon anyone found guilty of any crime. The only exception is people who have been impeached.

A VIEW FROM ABROAD

Alexis de Tocqueville of France visited the United States during the early 1830s. Tocqueville was a historian and political thinker. He wrote this about the U.S. presidency after returning to France:

"In America the President cannot prevent any law from being passed, nor can he evade the obligation of enforcing it.... All his important acts are directly or indirectly submitted to the legislature.... In Europe, harmony must reign between the crown and the other branches of the legislature, because a collision between them may prove serious; in America, the harmony is not indispensable, because such a collision is impossible."

Creating the Modern Presidency

Some presidents throughout history have pushed the limits of their power. Andrew Jackson and Abraham Lincoln were two strong 19th-century presidents. Jackson served from 1829 to 1837. He tried to reach out directly to voters and shape public opinion to his view of events. He hoped the voters would then convince their members of Congress to support him.

Lincoln claimed the need to take on more power because of the American Civil War (1861–1865). The South's attempt to leave the United States threatened the nation. He believed that he had the power to keep the Union whole and that it was his supreme duty under the Constitution.

The size of the executive branch grew to deal with such events as World War I, the Great Depression, and World War II. Franklin D. Roosevelt was president during most of the Depression and World War II.

A FIRSTHAND LOOK AT

THE EMANCIPATION PROCLAMATION

Abraham Lincoln issued the Emancipation Proclamation on January 1, 1863. The document freed slaves held in Southern states at war with the Union. Lincoln claimed the right to do this as part of his powers as commander in chief. The original document is now at the National Archives in Washington, D.C. See page 60 for a link to view the document online.

President Roosevelt (seated) created a cabinet, or group of advisers. This marked a change in the way the presidency functions, and continues today.

Some of his success was due to Congress's realizing the country faced economic collapse and foreign attack. Congress gave Roosevelt, and future presidents, a larger staff that answered only to him. Some people today believe that increased presidential powers are not what the original creators of the Constitution intended.

CHAPTER 4

THE JUDICIAL BRANCH

The justices of the Supreme Court head the country's judicial branch.

THE DELEGATES IN PHILADELPHIA agreed that there would be a judiciary. It would have a supreme court and other lower courts. The president would choose judges. The Senate would approve them. The delegates also decided to give the judges their jobs for life.

The Constitution outlines what kinds of cases federal courts can hear. The cases must involve a federal law, international issues, or legal battles between two states or between one state and the federal government. Congress has the power to set the rules for the federal courts. The president could veto any proposal the lawmakers suggested. This gives the legislative and executive branches another shared power over the judiciary.

William Marbury's struggle to hold on to a position in the government led to an increase in the Supreme Court's power.

The Supreme Court

Decisions made in the lower federal courts can be appealed, or sent to a higher court for review. The decisions of the U.S. Supreme Court are final. But Congress can pass laws to get around specific points of a court decision. The Supreme Court might find a law unconstitutional if it is not written carefully.

The process of examining whether or not a law is constitutional is called judicial review. Judicial review is the Supreme Court's most important duty. The idea came out of the 1803 case of *Marbury v. Madison*. The case involved whether William Marbury would be allowed to fill a government position he received just before John Adams left the presidency. Thomas Jefferson was the next president. He did not want Marbury in the job. Chief Justice John Marshall wrote that Marbury should get the job. But his more important action was saying that a federal law that applied to the case was in conflict with the Constitution. The *Marbury* decision and judicial review gave the Supreme Court a larger role to play in shaping the government and American society.

Marshall's decision in *Marbury* set a precedent, or action that future courts would follow. The Supreme Court would have to reject a law that violated the Constitution. Judicial review also involves examining state laws and legal decisions to see if they conflict with the Constitution.

SPOTLIGHT ON

Chief Justice John Marshall

John Marshall (1755–1835) was a Virginian Federalist who wanted to strengthen the national government. His time on the Supreme Court helped to strengthen the judicial branch. He did this by introducing the concept of judicial review and having justices release just one decision. Judges released separate opinions under English custom. Marshall's method helped give the decision extra weight in the public's eye, since the court was speaking with a united voice. Justices today often release a number of separate opinions along with the court's overall decision.

Unpopular Decisions

Some Americans believe that Supreme Court justices often interpret certain constitutional phrases or clauses too broadly. This can be seen as a desire to make laws rather than interpret existing ones. This is called judicial activism. Courts can also follow judicial restraint. This is when they decide not to get involved in cases that are really Congress's to decide.

During the 1930s, President Franklin D. Roosevelt worked to create new government programs that would help repair the damage caused by the Great Depression. The court thought some of Roosevelt's New Deal programs were unconstitutional.

The Supreme Court's decision to end segregation in schools in 1954 inspired both criticism and celebration.

Roosevelt asked Congress in 1937 to increase the number of justices on the Supreme Court. His goal was to name new people more likely to support the New Deal. Many Americans viewed this as an attempt to weaken the judiciary's check on presidential and legislative power. Roosevelt failed to win support for his plan.

In 1954, Americans were outraged by the Supreme Court's unanimous decision in *Brown v. Board of Education*. Chief Justice Earl Warren wrote that states and towns could not segregate, or keep separate, white and black students by building separate schools for them. Critics said the court had given itself too much power by calling an end to segregation. Two southern

YESTERDAY'S HEADLINES

On February 8, 1937, the *New York Herald-Tribune* had this to say about Roosevelt's plan to add more justices:

"President Roosevelt has brought forward a proposal which, if enacted into law, would end the American State.... No President of the United States ever before made the least gesture toward attempting to gain such a vast grant of power.... By one legislative act, availing himself of the one loophole in the Constitution—the failure to specify the number of members in the Supreme Court—he would strike at the roots of that equality of the three branches of government."

Chief Justice Warren knew the decision in *Brown v. Board of Education* was historic. He read his decision to the court and the world. Justices rarely do this. The copy of the decision he read is now kept at the Manuscript Division of the Library of Congress. So are many other documents relating to the case. See page 60 for a link to view the decision online.

senators argued that the Constitution never mentions education. They believed that it was an issue that should be handled at the state level.

Recent Supreme Court decisions still fuel anger. The court ruled in 2010 that businesses have the same rights as people under the First Amendment. Five justices voted

Earl Warren (front row, center) and his fellow justices struck a major blow against segregation.

Elena Kagan represented the Federal Election Commission in the 2010 Supreme Court case.

for this ruling. Four voted against it. This decision in *Citizens United v. Federal Election Commission* meant that companies have a right to give as much money as they want to support political candidates, just as individuals do. Many people thought that candidates who lacked the support of wealthy companies would have a harder time getting elected. But U.S. courts are supposed to follow precedents. They base their decisions on how other courts decided similar cases in the past. The court rejected two earlier precedents in the *Citizens United* decision.

The decisions of the Supreme Court impact all areas of life. Sometimes they preserve the freedom of some Americans while limiting the desires and freedoms of others.

CHAPTER 5

BALANCING THE BRANCHES

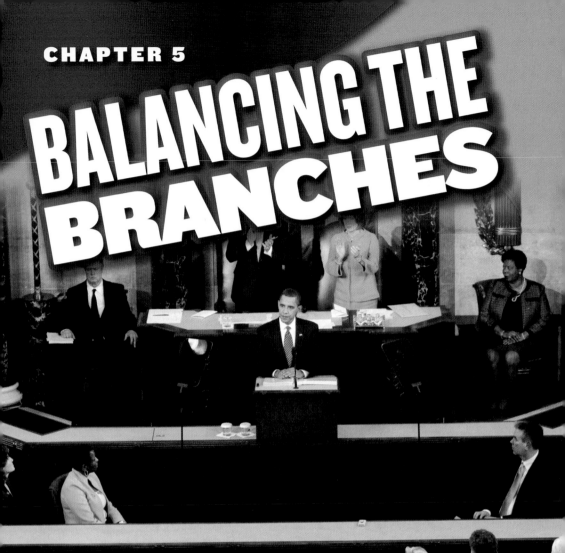

The three branches work together to accomplish the nation's goals.

The writers of the

Constitution were concerned with balancing the power of the three government branches. This means the branches share power. At times, one branch might try to do something that it believes is part of its constitutional power. But another branch might disagree.

The Vietnam War was a long and bloody conflict.

Warring over War Powers

Since the Korean War in 1950, the United States
has often fought in wars without Congress officially
declaring war. Presidents have claimed they can send
troops to battle under their powers as commander in
chief. Congress has accepted the presidents' actions in
these cases. But some lawmakers and other Americans
have challenged executive branch actions relating to this
and other war efforts. This happened to President Harry
Truman.

Workers in the steel industry threatened to go on
strike during the Korean War. They refused to work until
they received higher pay. President Truman said the steel
they made was crucial to the war effort. He wanted the
government to take control of the steel mills and keep

them running. The owners of the mills took the government to court. The Supreme Court ruled the case of *Youngstown, Sheet & Tube Co. v. Sawyer* in the owners' favor. The vote was six to three. The court claimed that Congress would have granted the president the power to take control of a company in earlier laws if it had wanted him to have such power.

In 1964, Congress voted to give President Lyndon Johnson wide power to carry out a war in South Vietnam. The lawmakers themselves did not declare war. Congress passed the War Powers Act after the troops left Vietnam in 1973. This law limited how long the president could send troops into a war zone without permission from Congress.

Critics thought the War Powers Act was an unconstitutional check on the president's power.

SPOTLIGHT ON

The War Powers Act

In 1999, several congressmen wanted the federal courts to rule that President Bill Clinton had violated the War Powers Act. The president ordered U.S. planes to bomb parts of Serbia that year. Serbia was carrying out attacks on Kosovo, then a region within the country. Congress voted against declaring war and for denying the president the power to carry out military operations. But the bombing continued. A federal court ruled in favor of Clinton. It refused to consider if his actions had violated the law or his powers as commander in chief.

President Richard Nixon vetoed the bill. But Congress voted to overturn it. Most presidents since then have simply ignored the law.

Executive Power and the War on Terror

The September 11, 2001, al-Qaeda terrorist attack on the United States introduced Americans to a new kind of war. President George W. Bush believed his powers as commander in chief gave him the right to take many actions on his own. These included deciding who was a threat to the country and holding suspected terrorists in jail without bringing legal charges against them. Critics said Bush's actions violated the Constitution.

Many Americans disagreed with Bush's interpretation of his presidential powers.

Though he was a U.S. citizen, Yaser Esam Hamdi was held as an enemy combatant until the *Hamdi v. Rumsfeld* case was heard.

The Supreme Court agreed with the president's critics in several cases. In *Hamdi v. Rumsfeld* (2004) the court ruled with a vote of five to four that a U.S. citizen who was fighting in Afghanistan against the United States could not be denied his constitutional right to a lawyer or a trial.

The court limited presidential power again two years later. In *Hamdan v. Rumsfeld,* the court struck down the use of a military court, rather than regular courts,

YESTERDAY'S HEADLINES

In 2009, President Barack Obama supported a law that changed the nature of the military commissions. The *Christian Science Monitor* reported:

"The 2009 law retains the basic structure of the existing commissions. A military judge presides over the trial.... and a panel of US service members decides issues of fact and guilt or innocence.... Opponents of military commissions say that the federal court system in the United States is robust enough to prosecute Al Qaeda suspects. 'The Military Commissions Act of 2009 raises serious constitutional concerns,' said Virginia Sloan, president of the Constitution Project. . . . 'The reformed commissions still fail to provide critical safeguards for the accused.'"

to decide if Salim Ahmed Hamdan had broken the law. The vote had been five to three against the use of military courts. Hamdan had worked in Afghanistan as a driver for al-Qaeda leader Osama bin Laden. Congress then passed a law that let the president continue using military commissions instead of courts to try some terrorists.

The Greatest Challenge Ever?

To some historians, the greatest challenge to the Constitution and the separation of powers came in 1974. Two years before, people working for President Richard

The Watergate building was the first scene in the scandal that ruined President Nixon's reputation among many U.S. citizens.

Nixon were caught committing burglary. Nixon knew about the crime but lied about what he knew. He tried to prevent the Federal Bureau of Investigation from investigating the crime. The burglary took place at a building in Washington, D.C., called the Watergate. The incident became known by that name.

Nixon turned over the Watergate tapes in April 1974.

Congress began its own investigation of Watergate. It learned that Nixon had secretly recorded many conversations at the White House. A lawyer helping the investigators demanded that the president turn over the tapes. Nixon refused. He claimed what is called executive privilege. He said the president does not have to provide all information the other branches ask for.

The Supreme Court disagreed. The president does have some claim to executive privilege, especially to

A FIRSTHAND LOOK AT
THE NIXON TAPES

Richard Nixon was not the first president to record meetings and phone calls in the White House. But his recordings are the most famous presidential tapes. More than 2,600 hours of taped conversations are available to the public. Researchers can listen to them at the Nixon Library in Yorba Linda, California. See page 60 for a link to hear the tapes online.

protect information that could harm the nation if it was released. But the Supreme Court has the power to decide how broad the privilege is. Nixon turned over the tapes, which proved his role in Watergate. Nixon resigned as the House was preparing to impeach him. He was the only president to leave office while facing impeachment.

Richard Nixon resigned from the presidency on August 9, 1974.

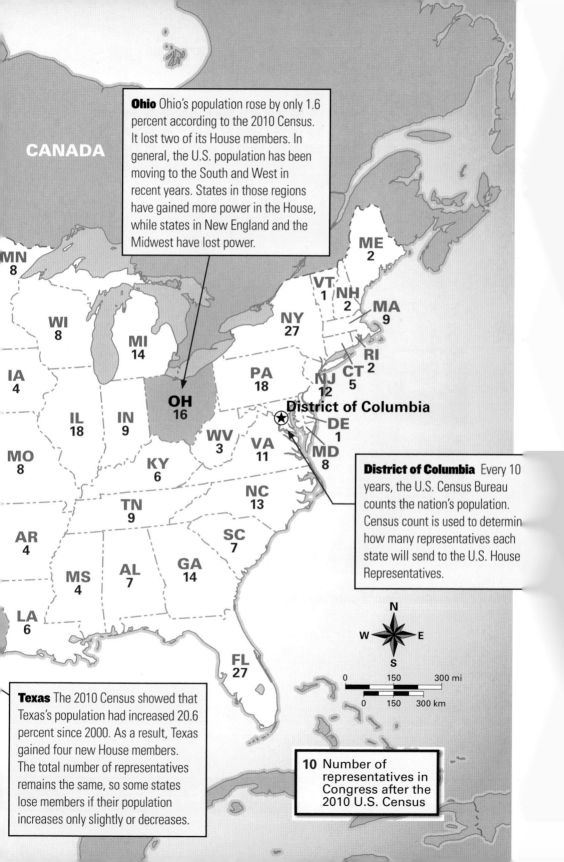

CANADA

Ohio Ohio's population rose by only 1.6 percent according to the 2010 Census. It lost two of its House members. In general, the U.S. population has been moving to the South and West in recent years. States in those regions have gained more power in the House, while states in New England and the Midwest have lost power.

MN
8

ME
2

VT
1

NH
2

MA
9

NY
27

WI
8

MI
14

RI
2

CT
5

IA
4

PA
18

NJ
12

OH
16

IL
18

IN
9

WV
3

VA
11

DE
1

MD
8

District of Columbia

MO
8

KY
6

NC
13

TN
9

SC
7

AR
4

MS
4

AL
7

GA
14

LA
6

FL
27

District of Columbia Every 10 years, the U.S. Census Bureau counts the nation's population. Census count is used to determin how many representatives each state will send to the U.S. House Representatives.

N
W E
S

0   150   300 mi

0   150   300 km

Texas The 2010 Census showed that Texas's population had increased 20.6 percent since 2000. As a result, Texas gained four new House members. The total number of representatives remains the same, so some states lose members if their population increases only slightly or decreases.

10 Number of representatives in Congress after the 2010 U.S. Census

The Branches Today

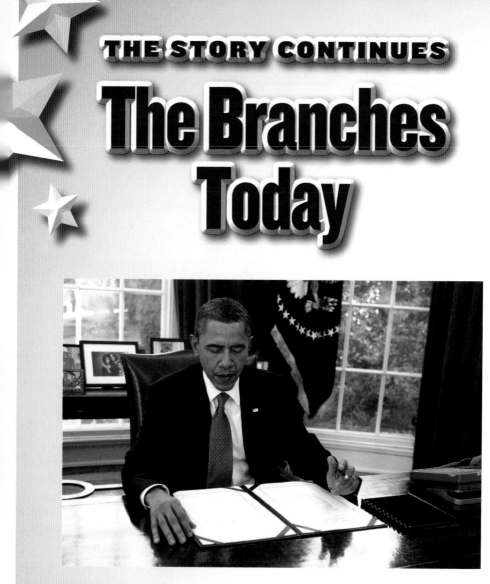

Presidents must carefully consider each new law that is brought before them.

Conflicts between the branches still arise. Presidents still claim executive privilege so they do not have to release certain information. They also issue signing statements when signing a bill into law. In these statements, presidents claim the right to not enforce the parts of a law that they think are unconstitutional. Congress has considered bills that would prevent a president from issuing these statements. Congress believes that presidents should veto a law if they find it unconstitutional instead of saying which parts will be enforced and which will be ignored. This issue could cause a future battle between the executive and the other two branches.

The three branches manage to work together despite the conflicts. They address the complex needs of a large nation and preserve the freedoms laid out in the Constitution.

The three branches work hard to overcome differences and provide effective leadership for the nation.

44TH U.S. PRESIDENT IN 2009.

George Washington

John Adams

George Washington (1732–1799) tried to make the federal government as strong as possible, and he took decisive action to end the Whiskey Rebellion in Pennsylvania.

John Adams (1735–1826) was a lawyer who believed strongly in the separation of powers. In 1796, he was elected the second U.S. president.

James Madison (1751–1836) has been called the Father of the Constitution, as he suggested many of the ideas that became part of it. He also wrote most of the amendments that formed the Bill of Rights. He served as the fourth president of the United States.

Alexander Hamilton (ca. 1755–1804) fought bravely during the American Revolution and then became a leader in the effort to create a stronger national government. He was killed in a pistol duel with Vice President Aaron Burr.

Franklin D. Roosevelt (1882–1945) expanded the power of the president during times of crisis. He failed in his effort to add new justices to the Supreme Court, seeking to name people who would support his policies.

Earl Warren (1891–1974) upset many Americans who thought that he, as chief justice, and his fellow justices were practicing judicial activism. He wrote the historic decision that said schools could not segregate students based on their race.

Richard Nixon (1913–1994) clashed with Congress, claiming the right to withhold information that lawmakers wanted. The Supreme Court ruled against him, and he resigned.

George W. Bush (1946–) claimed many powers in his role as commander in chief, in order to fight the war on terror. The Supreme Court struck down some of his actions, though Congress usually supported him.

George W. Bush

TIMELINE

1775

The American Revolutionary War begins.

1776

Americans declare their independence from Great Britain.

1781

Ratification of the Articles of Confederation creates the first national U.S. government.

1783

The Revolutionary War ends, and the United States wins its independence.

1861

Declaring that states do not have a constitutional right to secede, Abraham Lincoln leads the Union into the American Civil War.

1913

The 17th Amendment gives voters the right to elect their U.S. senators.

1937

Franklin D. Roosevelt tries to add new justices to the U.S. Supreme Court.

1951

The 22nd Amendment limits a U.S. president to two terms in office.

1787

Delegates in Philadelphia write the U.S. Constitution, creating a new government for the country.

1788

The Constitution is ratified.

1791

The Bill of Rights is ratified.

1803

In *Marbury v. Madison*, Chief Justice John Marshall declares the Supreme Court's power to decide if laws are unconstitutional.

1954

Chief Justice Earl Warren and his court declare segregation unconstitutional.

1973

The War Powers Act limits how long a president can send U.S. troops into battle without permission from Congress.

1974

The U.S. Supreme Court denies President Nixon's claim of executive privilege.

2004

The U.S. Supreme Court rules against George W. Bush, saying his powers as commander in chief do not give him the right to deny a U.S. citizen certain basic legal rights.

LIVING HISTORY

Primary sources provide firsthand evidence about a topic. Witnesses to a historical event create primary sources. They include autobiographies, newspaper reports of the time, oral histories, photographs, and memoirs. A secondary source analyzes primary sources, and is one step or more removed from the event. Secondary sources include textbooks, encyclopedias, and commentaries.

Articles of Confederation The Articles of Confederation can be viewed online at the Library of Congress Web site. Check them out at *http://memory.loc.gov/cgi-bin/ampage?collId=rbpe&fileName=rbpe17/ rbpe178/17802600/rbpe17802600.db&recNum=0*

The Emancipation Proclamation The original Emancipation Proclamation is kept at the National Archives in Washington, D.C., but you can read a copy online by visiting *www.archives.gov/exhibits /featured_documents/emancipation_proclamation/*

Nixon Presidential Library and Museum The Nixon Library in Yorba Linda, California, has a variety of materials relating to Nixon's life and presidency. These include photos, film clips, and his White House tapes. Much of this information is available online at *www. nixonlibrary.gov/virtuallibrary/index.php*

U.S. Capitol Exhibition Hall Exhibition Hall is part of the visitors' center at the Capitol, where Congress meets. It features an exhibit on the history of Congress and the Capitol itself. Part of the exhibit looks at the Constitution and the role of the three branches of the federal government. For more information, visit *www.visitthecapitol.gov /Exhibitions/online/*

The Warren Decision You can view a copy of Justice Warren's decision on *Brown v. Board of Education* on the Library on Congress Web site by visiting *www.loc.gov/exhibits/brown/brown-brown.html*

RESOURCES

Books

Elish, Dan. *The U.S. Supreme Court*. New York: Children's Press, 2007.

Fradin, Dennis Brindell. *The U.S. Constitution*. New York: Marshall Cavendish Books, 2008.

Taylor-Butler, Christine. *The Presidency*. New York: Children's Press, 2008.

Zurlo, Tony. *The Legislative Branch: Creating America's Laws*. Berkeley Heights, NJ: MyReportLinks.com Books, 2008.

Web Sites

Supreme Court of the United States

www.supremecourt.gov

Visit the official Supreme Court Web site to learn more about current and past justices, as well as decisions dating back to 1991.

United States House of Representatives

www.house.gov

Check out the official House Web site to keep track of current bills and see how members have voted on past bills.

United States Senate

www.senate.gov

Visit the official Senate Web site to find out more about current and past senators and read speeches they have given.

The White House—Our Government

www.whitehouse.gov/our-government

The president's official Web site explains how federal, state, and local governments work, with a look at all three federal branches and the Constitution.

GLOSSARY

amendments (uh-MEND-muhnts) changes that are made to a law or a legal document

bills (BILLZ) written plans for new laws

budget (BUHJ-it) a plan for how money will be spent

delegates (DEL-i-gitz) representatives to a convention or congress

executive (eg-ZEK-yuh-tiv) the branch of government that carries out laws

federal (FED-ur-uhl) referring to a system of government that balances power between states and the national government, or another name for the national government

judicial (joo-DISH-uhl) relating to the court system

legislative (LEJ-iss-lay-tiv) relating to the branch of government that makes laws

majority (muh-JOR-uh-tee) half the members of a group plus one

nominees (nom-uh-NEEZ) people chosen as candidates by a political party or an office holder

partisan (PAR-tih-zun) strongly pursuing the views or goals of one political party

ratify (RAT-uh-fye) to approve, such as a legal document

vetoes (VEE-tohz) stops a bill from becoming a law

INDEX

Page numbers in *italics* indicate illustrations.

ABOUT THE AUTHOR

Michael Burgan has written more than 250
books for children and young adults, including
fiction and nonfiction. He specializes in U.S.
history and has written many books on colonial
America, the American Revolution, and the
founding of the nation. He graduated from the
University of Connecticut with a degree in history
and has won several awards for his work.